Lilies
or
The Revival of a Romantic
Drama

Lilies
or
The Revival of a Romantic Drama

Michel Marc Bouchard

Translated by Linda Gaboriau

Playwrights Canada Press
Toronto • Canada

Lilies, English Translation © Linda Gaboriau, 1990

Playwrights Canada Press
54 Wolseley St., 2nd fl. Toronto, Ontario CANADA M5T 1A5
Tel: (416) 703-0201 Fax: (416) 703-0059
e-mail: cdplays@interlog.com   http://www.puc.ca

Originally published in French as [Les Feleuttes ou la Répétition d'un drama romantique]
by Leméac Éditeur, Montreal, © 1987

Translator's Note: For the benefit of readers who might wish to compare this translation with the original aspublished by Leméac Éditeur, it is important to Note that, at the playwright's request, the translation is based on the script as it was revised for production., Certain lines were rewritten and others cut

Playwrights Canada Press publishes with the generous assistance of The Canada Council for the arts- Writing and Publishing Section and the Ontario Arts Council.

Cover design by Stephanie Power / Reactor. Cover Illustration: Saint Sebastion (Andrea Mantegna), courtesy of Kunsthistoriches Museum, Vienna. Playwright photo by Robert Laliberté.

Canadian Cataloguing in Publication Data
Bouchard, Michel Marc, 1958 —
        [Les Feluettes, ou, la répétition d'un drame romantique. English]
        Lilies, or, The revival of a romantic drama
A play.
Translation of Les feluettes, ou, la répétition d'un drame romantique.
ISBN 0-88754-545-9

I. Gaboriau, Linda.   I.Title.   II. Title: The revival of a romantic dream.

PS8553.07745F4413 1997   C842'.54   C97-932075-5
PQ3919.2.B5855F4413 1997

First edition: 1990 (Coach House Press).
Playwrights Canada Press First Printing: September, 1997
Playwrights Canada Press Second Printing: November, 1998
Playwrights Canada Press Third Printing: March 2000
Printed and bound by Hignell Printing at Winnipeg, Manitoba

"What is vice?—Those sins we commit without pleasure."
COLETTE

… In memory of Claude Jutra

… For Benoit Lagrandeur

… For my mother

Les Feluettes ou La Répétition d'un drame romantique was first performed at Salle Fred-Barry, in Montreal, on September 10, 1987, with the following cast:

Jean Archambault	*Monseigneur Bilodeau*
Jean-François Blanchard	*Le comte Vallier de Tilly*
René Richard Cyr	*Jean Bilodeau*
Hubert Gagnon	*Le vieux Simon, Le père Saint-Michel, Le baron de Hüe*
René Gagnon	*La comtesse Marie-Laure de Tilly*
Claude Godbout	*L'étudiant, La baronne de Hüe*
Yves Jacques	*Mademoiselle Lydie-Anne de Rozier*
Roger Larue	*Timothée Doucet*
Denis Roy	*Simon Doucet*

Directed by André Brassard
Assisted by Lou Fortier
Set design by Richard Lacroix
Costumes by Marc-André Coulombe
Lighting by Claude Accolas
Music by Christian Thomas

This production was co-produced by Théâtre Petit à Petit (Montreal) and Théâtre français du Centre national des Arts (Ottawa).

John Gilbert	*Bishop Bilodeau*
Leonard Chow	*Count Vallier*
Duncan Ollerenchaw	*Jean Bilodeau*
*	*Simon Doucet in 1912*
*	*Father Saint-Michel, Baron de Hüe*
Richard Partington	*Countess Marie-Laure de Tilly*
Neil Barclay	*Student, Baroness de Hüe*
Maurice Godin	*Mademoiselle Lydie-Anne de Rozier*
John Dolan	*Timothée Doucet, Simon in 1952*

Directed by Brian Richmond
Assisted by Sally Han
Set design and costumes by Leslie Frankish
Lighting by Steven Hawkins
Music by Don Horsburgh
Stage manager: Aaron Moses

* Not cast at time of publication.

The English-language production of *Lilies or The Revival of a Romantic Drama* premiered at Theatre Passe Muraille on February 1, 1991, with the follow cast:

John Gilbert	*Bishop Bilodeau*
Leonard Chow	*Count Vallier*
Duncan Ollerenchaw	*Jean Bilodeau*
*	*Simon Doucet in 1912*
*	*Father Saint-Michel, Baron de Hüe*
Richard Partington	*Countess Marie-Laure de Tilly*
Neil Barclay	*Student, Baroness de Hüe*
Maurice Godin	*Mademoiselle Lydie-Anne de Rozier*
John Dolan	*Timothée Doucet, Simon in 1952*

Directed by Brian Richmond
Assisted by Sally Han
Set design and costumes by Leslie Frankish
Lighting by Steven Hawkins

Reflections on the Shore of an Inner Sea

I lived in Roberval in 1912 ... three years ago. I walked through the smoke of the sawmill in the north of the city ... there where, years before, people had lingered on the main terrace of the Hôtel Roberval. I stood there and contemplated the same landscape that they had admired in those days ... an immense expanse of calm water and the calm, azure sky.... My task was to paint onto this landscape a naïve love story which never could have existed outside such silence and isolation.

That is when I met Vallier and Simon.... I mistook them for Angélique, Marquise des Anges, and Geoffroy, from a sentimental television series that was being re-re-rebroadcast on the regional network.

I met the Countess.... I mistook her for my own inability to adapt to reality.

I saw Lydie-Anne hovering over the water.... I mistook her balloon for the perfect red sphere the summer sunsets cast upon the lake, and then disappear like an illusion.

A crow flew by, and I mistook it for Bilodeau....

But then, I still mistake nobility and betrayal, courage and cowardice.

Of all these hallucinations, only the timeless witnesses remained—water, earth, fire and air. They became the raw materials of my story.

Like those characters who long to escape their reality, like Simon in 1952, who wants to know the end of his drama, like the sadomasochistic Saint Sebastian who longs to die, that he might be reborn ... I too tried to drown in the waters of this inner sea, so that I might believe in this love story that no one ever told me.

It begins like this....

Michel Marc Bouchard
September, 1987

Dramatis Personae

Nine to twelve men playing....

In 1912:

SIMON DOUCET. A young Québécois, born in Roberval. Impulsive by nature. A pyromaniac. Known for his exceptional beauty. His father's pride and joy. He is nineteen.

COUNT VALLIER DE TILLY. A young Frenchman, has recently made Roberval his home. A direct descendant of the Bourbons. Known for his intelligence, but also for his delicate manners and excessive sensitivity which have earned him the nickname Lily-White. He is several months younger than Simon.

FATHER SAINT-MICHEL. Has been teaching for four years at Saint Sebastian's School for Boys where he is currently directing a production of *The Martyrdom of Saint Sebastian*. His theatrical endeavors with ecclesiastical–erotic overtones are beginning to make tongues wag.

JEAN BILODEAU. A young man from Roberval. Studies at the boys' school and has a role in Father Saint-Michel's production.

A YOUNG STUDENT. Jean Bilodeau's replacement in the role of the Syrian slave girl in Father Saint-Michel's production.

COUNTESS MARIE-LAURE DE TILLY. A distinguished woman in her fifties. Vallier's mother. When she is not lost in her fantasies or settling her differences of opinion with her only son, she is awaiting the return of her husband who left on a trip to France five years before.

TIMOTHÉE DOUCET. In his fifties, born in Roberval. Alcoholic. Widower. Simon's father. He has been Vallier's footman on Wednesdays for the past six years.

BARON DE HÜE. A French doctor, vacationing at the Hôtel Roberval.

MADEMOISELLE LYDIE-ANNE DE ROZIER. A Frenchwoman in her early thirties, very attractive. Owner of an aerostat. Over the years she has become an expert liar.

BARONESS DE HÜE. The baron's wife. Enjoys the outdoors and has a weak spot for ouananich salmon fishing.

In 1952:

SIMON IN 1952.

HIS EXCELLENCY BISHOP JEAN BILODEAU.

Prologue

Spring of 1952.
A proscenium stage. We hear someone entering in the dark.

BISHOP BILODEAU: Is there anyone here? Mr. Doucet? Are you there? [*Silence.*] Answer me if you're there!

SIMON IN 1952: Why, is that His Excellency Bishop Jean Bilodeau? You're an hour late, Your Excellency.

BISHOP BILODEAU: I did what I could. [*They look at each other silently. The* BISHOP *lowers his eyes repeatedly.*] It's not easy for a bishop to find time for a personal appointment. [*Silence.*] You ... you haven't changed much.

SIMON IN 1952: You have. You look old.

BISHOP BILODEAU: I brought some information on the different rehabilitation programs the Church offers ex-prisoners. I thought it might be of use to you. [*Silence.*] I don't have much time to spare. I'd like to know the purpose of this meeting, Mr. Doucet?

SIMON IN 1952: You can drop the "Mr. Doucet." All those years in prison, I fell asleep every night dreaming of the day you'd look me in the eye and call me by my name again. "Simon."

BISHOP BILODEAU: That was a long time ago, Mr. Doucet. We are no longer students. Our lives have led us along very different paths. The fact that yours hasn't treated you too kindly.... Why were you so determined to see me again? [*Silence.*] If you think you were the victim of an error, I hardly see how I can right the wrongs of the judicial system. I am a bishop. Speak to a judge.

SIMON IN 1952: For years I went around protesting that I was innocent. I begged them to call you back to testify again, but you were untouchable. Mr. Bilodeau was preparing to enter the priesthood. [*Impulsively.*] You might have forgotten, but I haven't. It's engraved in my mind, my flesh, in my heart, in my soul.... All the dirty things you said about me....

Noise in the background.

BISHOP BILODEAU: Is there someone else here? You promised this meeting would be private!

SIMON IN 1952: They're friends. Some old acquaintances from our days at the boys' school in Roberval.

The curtain rises. We can make out the silhouettes of some ten men.

BISHOP BILODEAU [*panicking*]: Who are these men? What are you going to do to me? I am a man of the Church!

SIMON IN 1952 [*indicating who will be playing whom*]: You remember the Baron and the Baroness de Hüe? Father Saint-Michel? Lydie-Anne de Rozier, the wealthy heiress from Paris? Countess Marie-Laure de Tilly, a direct descendant of the Bourbons?

BISHOP BILODEAU: All these people are dead. You're being macabre, Mr. Doucet! This is ancient history. As outdated as the Countess de Tilly was at the time. This is absurd.

SIMON IN 1952: This young man is me; he's handsome the way people said I was in those days. This is Count Vallier de Tilly, the countess's son ... and that little sneak there is you.

BISHOP BILODEAU: I'm leaving.

SIMON IN 1952 *intercepts* BISHOP BILODEAU *and threatens him with a knife.*

SIMON IN 1952: They're all like me, victims of a judicial error. You know, you learn lots of things in prison ... even how to kill. We been workin' on our show for three years, just for you, Your Excellency. It would be a shame if you had to leave prematurely.... [*He releases* BISHOP BILODEAU.]

BISHOP BILODEAU: I have no idea what you're talking about!

SIMON IN 1952: I rotted in jail for years for something I never did! There's only one person in the world who knows what really happened one September morning in 1912.

BISHOP BILODEAU: Do you realize that you are holding a bishop hostage?

SIMON IN 1952: I just invited my old schoolmate to a little theatrical evening, like we used to organize back in those days. Oh, by the way, I'll be playing Timothée Doucet, my dear father.

BISHOP BILODEAU: Just what do you want from me?

SIMON IN 1952: For the time being, nothing. Just sit down and watch. Then ... we'll see.... [*The actors take their places.*] In the spring of 1912, you must remember, back at the school in Roberval, we were rehearsing *The Martyrdom of Saint Sebastian* by the Italian poet, Gabriele D'Annunzio.... I was Saint Sebastian. Sanaé, the saint's friend, was being played by Count de Tilly, the one you had nicknamed Lily-White.

Episode 1

Late May 1912.
The rehearsal hall at Saint Sebastian's School for Boys in Roberval.
In the background, the music Debussy wrote for The Martyrdom
of Saint Sebastian. *The set consists of a painted backdrop depict-*
ing a Roman landscape in the later period of antiquity. One can dis-
tinguish the façade of a temple, some hills and vineyards. Placed in
front of the backdrop is a spindly tree.

VALLIER [*playing* SANAÉ]: Caesar said: "Take him to Apollo's
Wood; tie him to the trunk of the finest bay tree; then let
your arrows fly into his naked body until your quivers are
empty, until his naked body is like that of a wild hedgehog."

SIMON [*playing* SEBASTIAN]: Yes, Sanaé, yes, my archers, that is
my desire. It shall be beautiful. [*He takes a rope and goes over*
to the spindly tree meant to be the finest bay tree. He hands the
rope to SANAÉ.] It shall be beautiful.

VALLIER [*playing* SANAÉ, *in despair*]: But Caesar said: "Then cut
his beautiful locks and place them on the altar, as a sign of
atonement. That I may shed my tears upon them." [*Enthusi-*
astically.] Might we simply cut some woman's hair and take
it to the Emperor?

SIMON [*playing* SEBASTIAN]: I shall be reborn, Sanaé. But that I
may be reborn, oh, my archers, I must die. I must die.

VALLIER [*playing* SANAÉ]: We shall break our bows.

SIMON [*playing* SEBASTIAN]: Draw your bows! Where is your
love for me? You love me, and you desire nothing more than
to serve my fate, yet you would obstruct the fulfillment of
my destiny and the completion of this cycle of my eternity.
You love me, yet you do not exalt in my mystery. I say unto
you, I shall be reborn. Have no fear. Verily, I assure you.

VALLIER [*playing* SANAÉ]: My Lord, we shall be killing our love.

SIMON: If you do truly love me....

THE STUDENT, *playing* THE SYRIAN SLAVE GIRL, *enters suddenly and*
exuberantly.

THE STUDENT [*playing* THE SYRIAN SLAVE GIRL]: He is dying, the beautiful Adonis. Weep! Weep! He is dead, the beautiful Adonis. Weep! Weep!

FATHER SAINT-MICHEL: Too soon! Too soon for the young Syrian slave girl. Go back to the wings.

THE STUDENT: I can't hear a thing in the wings. I don't mind re-placing Jean Bilodeau, but just don't yell at me!

FATHER SAINT-MICHEL: Back to the wings, please!

THE STUDENT *returns to the wings.*

SIMON: Isn't somebody supposed to tie me up?

FATHER SAINT-MICHEL: The archers of Emesa are.... But....

SIMON [*furious*]: So where are the archers?

FATHER SAINT-MICHEL: They're late, like Jean Bilodeau.

VALLIER: We haven't seen him for almost a week....

SIMON: Why do they havta tie up Saint Sebastian anyway? He's the last one who'd try to get away. I never saw anyone want to die so bad.

FATHER SAINT-MICHEL: It's to prevent his body from falling when he's hit by the arrows.

SIMON: He thought of everything. He really wants to die!

FATHER SAINT-MICHEL: He wants to die to escape eternal dark-ness, Simon. A man who truly believes in something can conquer the unconquerable, even death. Please continue.

VALLIER *ties* SIMON *to the tree.*

SIMON [*playing* SEBASTIAN]: A man must kill his love, that it may be reborn seven times more ardent. Oh, my archers, archers, if you do truly love me, let your love ... be known unto me by the pain of your arrows.

FATHER SAINT-MICHEL: That's when Sanaé throws himself upon his master's body. Like Mary Magdalene upon Jesus, like Lazarus on Our Lord.

VALLIER *throws himself awkwardly, limply, onto* SIMON.

FATHER SAINT-MICHEL: I meant Lazarus, *after* his resurrection! You
fall on him like a corpse. I realize such signs of affection are
not very common in Roberval, but Saint Sebastian is your
love, and he is asking you to kill him. Just imagine, the person
you love most in the world asking you such a favor [*corrects
himself*] ... such a sacrifice. It's a moment of ultimate love!

SIMON: Is that where the arrows come in?

FATHER SAINT-MICHEL: Yes. But I haven't decided how we're
going to manage the arrows. It's merely a detail. Carry on!

SIMON [*amazed*]: Twenty-two arrows shot at someone from ten
feet away. You call that a detail!?

VALLIER: You said the same thing last year about Saint Alphonse's ascension. The poor martyr ended up at the doctor's because the doors of heaven refused to open! The
saint's descent got more applause than all his passion.

FATHER SAINT-MICHEL: It's hardly the same situation. We were
unable to rehearse that detail. Carry on!

SIMON: There's only seven days to go before our deputy comes
from Quebec City to give us our diplomas.

FATHER SAINT-MICHEL: Will you simply concentrate on the text,
my children. Deliver it with as much fervor as possible.

SIMON: Do you really think the deputy's going to like our performance? Boys caressing each other and smooching on
stage. I'm not sure people around here are gonna like it.
When I ran my fingers through Vallier's hair last year....

VALLIER: I was a horse. It's not the same.

SIMON: That's what I mean. You were just a horse, but for a few
minutes there it felt like the audience lost their taste for rid-
ing. [*Notices that* FATHER SAINT-MICHEL *is hurt.*] I'm sorry.

VALLIER: Simon didn't mean to hurt your feelings, Father Saint-
Michel.

FATHER SAINT-MICHEL: The fact is, he's right. No one understands
me. I try to offer them modern productions. But I keep for-
getting that we are at the mercy of an audience of peasants

whose taste is limited to operettas, light comedies or melo-dramas. And the clergy is only interested in seeing saints stoned to death, impaled, burned at the stake, carved into pieces ... served as hors d'œuvres with spicy sauces. I feel utterly defeated. That's it, utterly defeated. I'll repeat that to myself until I finally accept my defeat. I feel utterly defeated.

VALLIER: But there are people who appreciate what you're doing. The Brother Superior.... The Indians always laugh.

FATHER SAINT-MICHEL [*slightly offended*]: Vallier!

VALLIER: My mother wouldn't miss one of your productions for anything in the world.

FATHER SAINT-MICHEL: Of course, there are a few aristocrats like Madame the Countess who know how to appreciate such things. But theater should reach everyone. One can do any-thing in the theater, you know. One can reinvent life. One can be in love, jealous, insane, tyrannical or possessed. One can even lie and cheat. One can kill without feeling the slightest remorse. One can die of love, of hate, of passion....

VALLIER: One can conquer the unconquerable!

SIMON [*enthusiastically, playing* SEBASTIAN]: If you do truly love me....

THE STUDENT [*playing* THE SYRIAN SLAVE GIRL]: He is dying, the beautiful....

FATHER SAINT-MICHEL: Please go back to the wings....

THE STUDENT: If you're not satisfied, why don't you get Bilo-deau? He just showed up backstage.

FATHER SAINT-MICHEL: It's about time! You gentlemen can re-hearse the last scene of Saint Sebastian's martyrdom while I go arrange for Mr. Bilodeau's. [*To the student.*] Come along with me!

They exit.

VALLIER: Thus, I rush towards you, and, as if driven by a fiery passion hitherto unknown to me, I press your body to mine. [VALLIER *presses himself against* SIMON*'s body. Dropping the the-atrical tone.*] Tell me that you love me!

SIMON [*refusing to repeat after* VALLIER]: I feel good when I'm with you.

VALLIER: Tell me that you love me!!

SIMON: You remind me of a girl when you act like that. I hate it. "That I feel good with you!!"

VALLIER: ... That you've never felt so good with anyone else?

SIMON [*tenderly*]: That I never felt so good with anyone else ... in my whole life. [*Continues to exchange embraces and kisses with* VALLIER.] Oh the quaking of my soul! I can feel my soul and this tree quaking down to the tips of the most hidden roots.

BISHOP BILODEAU: I've seen enough! [*Authoritatively.*] I am willing to attend this performance as long as it remains within the limits of decency!

SIMON [*playing* SEBASTIAN]: Whom amongst you would I elect? He who takes aim with his most deadly arrow and releases it with such terrible force.... Verily I shall know that man loves me, and will always love me. Sanaé, do you have my bow? Press it to my lips before you draw it.... May it touch my lips and my soul.

BISHOP BILODEAU: You are making a caricature out of Father Saint-Michel. You make yourselves look like angels, guardians of the truth. You're coloring everything with perverse, erotic overtones. You're confusing moral virtue and pagan acts.

VALLIER *and* SIMON *embrace and kiss each other.*

SIMON IN 1952: You're the last one who should talk about morality.

SIMON [*playing* SEBASTIAN]: My destiny must be fulfilled. I must die at the hands of men.... Hurry!

Young BILODEAU *enters. Long silence.*

SIMON [*taunting him*]: C'mon, Bilodeau, say your lines. What are you waitin' for, Bilodeau?

FATHER SAINT-MICHEL [*re-entering*]: Mr. Bilodeau! [*Very gently.*] I was telling your classmates what a great adventure theater

is, an exalting adventure where one can re-create the world
... [*suddenly*] ... provided that the actors are present for the
rehearsals!

BILODEAU: I haven't been to rehearsal because my mother's for-
bidden me to come.... You're gonna have to find yourself
another slave.

FATHER SAINT-MICHEL: And why, may I ask?

BILODEAU: She tried to make my costume....

FATHER SAINT-MICHEL: What happened? She ran out of material?

BILODEAU [*arrogantly*]: No, she had too much left over. Her and
Mrs. Lavigne and Mrs. Scott got together to work on the costumes and ... and they decided "costume" was a big word
for what we're supposed to wear. They said that hell will
freeze over before they let their kids walk around on stage
half naked like that. Mrs. Lavigne calls your costumes
"filthy rags," Mrs. Scott says they're "pervert's panties," and
my mother calls them ... "crack-ticklers." So I won't be coming to rehearsal any more. Neither will Caesar or the archer
with the wanton eyes. And the way things are going you
might be missing a whole regiment of centurions, on top of
the angels that were already missing.

FATHER SAINT-MICHEL: Jean, come over here please. You have a
great deal of talent, Jean....

BILODEAU: My mother says you better not try to get me to come
back. Anyways, she says.... Forget it, she didn't say anything.

FATHER SAINT-MICHEL [*annoyed*]: I'd appreciate your finishing
your sentence, Mr. Bilodeau.

BILODEAU: I did finish. I got nothing else to say.

SIMON: Damn liar! You were gonna say something else. Let's
hear it. Tell us what Bilodeau's mummy said this time.

VALLIER: Now what has that harpy made up?

BILODEAU: Harpy! I don't even know what "harpy" means!
Anyway, my mother might be a "harpy," but yours is crazy.
You must understand what that means ... "crazy"?! Why
can't you talk like everyone else, damn foreigner? His lily-
white lordship shows up here without a cent, gets the

priests to pay for his education, steals our friends. And then he dares go around talkin' with his mouth puckered up like a hen's ass. Lousy imported snobs.

FATHER SAINT-MICHEL [*grabbing young* BILODEAU *by the neck*]: Just what did she have to say this time, your gossiping mother? You must understand what "gossip" means?

BILODEAU [*taunting* FATHER SAINT-MICHEL]: You're usually gentler than that with young boys. [FATHER SAINT-MICHEL *tightens his grip around young* BILODEAU'S *throat.*] She said the more performances you put on, the sicker you get, and some of the guys like Vallier and Simon are starting to catch your sickness. Mrs. Lavigne and Mrs. Scott say you're like the plague ... [FATHER SAINT-MICHEL *releases* BILODEAU] ... and when the plague hits somewhere, you either get rid of it, or you havta leave, yourself.

FATHER SAINT-MICHEL [*beside himself*]: What plague were those respectable ladies referring to, Mr. Bilodeau? [*Silence.*] What plague, Mr. Bilodeau?

BILODEAU: How should I know? Why don't you go ask them yourself, if you're brave enough. They're in there explaining your little problem to the principal right now.

FATHER SAINT-MICHEL: I refuse to let those old prudes destroy four years of work.

FATHER SAINT-MICHEL *exits.* BILODEAU *goes to follow him.*

SIMON [*intercepts* BILODEAU]: So, Bilodeau, we're sick, eh? Now that we're all alone, why dontcha tell us what sickness we got.

VALLIER: You said something about a plague? Strange, but I haven't noticed anything on my skin. Have you, Simon?

BILODEAU: It's not a sickness you can see on your skin. It's inside you. It burns inside you like ... the flames of hell. It's like ... hell on earth. When I came across the two of you up in the attic last week, I saw your sickness plain as can be. God made it rain fire and brimstone on Sodom and Gomorrah because of that. He said: "Let me never see another man

do it, because the same thing will happen all over again."
Just because of you and Father Saint-Michel, Roberval could
become another Sodom and Gomorrah. I told Father Saint-
Michel what I saw in the attic. He stared at me like ... the
Antichrist, my mother says Father Saint-Michel is the Antichrist. He listened to every word. And he kept sighing and
patting me and saying: "Be more precise, Bilodeau, more
precise." I talked to him about hell.... But he got me so con-
fused, I started to wonder who knows more about hell, him
or my mother.

SIMON: So you told your mother all about it too?

BILODEAU: You crazy?

VALLIER: Well, I talked to my mother about it and she had nothing to say, except that at my age it's natural to experience
what you call "hell."

BILODEAU: That doesn't count, your mother's crazy.

SIMON: You call Vallier's mother crazy once more, and I'm
gonna show you what hell's really like. Say you're sorry!
C'mon!

BILODEAU [bitterly]: Okay. Okay. I'm sorry. I'm sorry ... Lily-
White. [To VALLIER.] Lucky you've always got Simon to defend you, damn lily-livered sissy. How 'bout you, Simon?
Did you tell your father? I'm sure he'd be real happy to
know about it. Everyone thinks you two make such a fine
pair, but nobody suspects....

SIMON: Suspects what? What are you getting at, Bilodeau?

BILODEAU: Your sickness is that you do things with Vallier like
he was a girl. And he's so sick, he calls that love. [He laughs.]

SIMON: Aren't you gettin' a bit carried away, Bilodeau?

BILODEAU: Ask Lily-White what he told me when you left the attic.

SIMON: There's a helluva difference between the things you do
in the attic and....

BILODEAU: He said that when you have a lot of feeling for
someone and you can't explain it, that's what love is. And
that's how he feels about you. And he said you feel the same
way about him.

SIMON: Shut up, Bilodeau!

BILODEAU: Lily-White also says you don't even have to talk about it together, that whenever you have a fight, you and him, and you go off and set a fire somewhere, he always understands that you're suffering ... from "love."

SIMON [*exasperated*]: Okay, Bilodeau! That's enough!

BILODEAU: Father Saint-Michel's punishment is nothing compared to what's in store for the two of you.

SIMON: It shall be beautiful. It shall be very beautiful. I'm gonna show you the flames of hell, Bilodeau.

SIMON *grabs* BILODEAU *by the collar and pulls him over to the tree.*
SIMON *picks up the rope and hands it to* VALLIER *who ties up* BILODEAU.

BILODEAU: What do you think you're doing? What do you think you're doing? You're sick, both of you. I don't want to be sick like you.

SIMON *shuts him up by kissing him.*

VALLIER [*reciting loudly in order to drown out* BILODEAU's *whimpering*]: From the depths, I call upon your terrible love, from the darkest depths. Again! Your love! Again and again! Your eternal love!

THE COUNTESS *enters, alone.* SIMON *hurries off.*

THE COUNTESS [*applauding*]: Why did you stop? What a pity! It was so beautiful! Oh, I understand. [*To someone who is not there.*] I didn't need you to explain, Timothée. [*To the boys.*] You want it to be a surprise? Of course. Children, we are going to have an opening night the likes of which has never been seen in Roberval. Father Saint-Michel is terribly audacious in his productions. I love it. I do love it! Such a divine way to break the monotony!

VALLIER: Good evening, Mother!

THE COUNTESS: Good evening, my son the Count. Aren't you going to say good evening to me, Mr. Bilodeau? [*Silence.*] I think he is still caught up in his part. But which part are you playing? Simon was supposed to play Saint Sebastian. Which means it isn't the saint who is tied to the tree. What an ingenious man Father Saint-Michel is! He's not afraid to break all the theatrical conventions.

VALLIER *unties* BILODEAU. *As soon as he is free,* BILODEAU *runs off.*

THE COUNTESS: I'm afraid that poor young man has inherited all his mother's worst faults. No manners at all! I might say the same for your son, Timothée. Why did Simon run off like that? [*Pause.*] You seem worried, Vallier.
VALLIER: The rehearsal exhausted me. It was particularly hectic. You, on the other hand, look radiant.
THE COUNTESS: I have the most wonderful news to tell you. Timothée, a chair for the Count please! [VALLIER *goes to get the chair himself.*] Vallier? That's what Timothée is here for!
VALLIER: I've been acting all day, Madame. I feel the need for some reality.
THE COUNTESS [*feigning that she is hurt*]: You know how I hate it when you remind Timothée of his absence.

TIMOTHÉE *enters.*

TIMOTHÉE: You didn't wait for me! I stopped off at the Hôtel Roberval.
THE COUNTESS [*ironically*]: Really!
TIMOTHÉE: Baron de Hüe and his wife just arrived. I met them two years ago. I went on a fishing trip with the Baroness. Caught around ten of them ouananich salmon myself, but she didn't catch nothing.... So I promised the Baroness I'd show her how to go flycasting next time she come back these ways.
THE COUNTESS: Timothée!

TIMOTHÉE: I hope you're not too mad because I'm late. It's just that Wednesday's the hardest day for me to be at your service. I know it's the day the train comes from Quebec City, but I wish we could make it Mondays or even Fridays....

THE COUNTESS: Timothée, I beg of you, please keep your distance when you speak to me. It's like being in the middle of a distillery.

TIMOTHÉE: My apologies, Madame.

He brings VALLIER *a chair.*

VALLIER: What's the wonderful news, Mother?!

THE COUNTESS: I met Mademoiselle Lydie-Anne de Rozier, the young Parisian woman who arrived by balloon today.

VALLIER [*skeptical*]: A young Parisian woman in a balloon, Timothée?

TIMOTHÉE: Yes, sir. A *real* Parisian.

VALLIER: The kind one sees in one's *dreams* or....

THE COUNTESS [*insulted*]: No, Vallier! The kind one sees in *Paris*.

TIMOTHÉE: A pretty good-lookin' woman and a real lady too. She says she's a descendant of Pilasse Desrosiers.

THE COUNTESS: Pilatre, Timothée. François Pilatre de Rozier, Timothée. Pilatre de Rozier is one of the inventors of the aerostat ... of balloons, Timothée. That is why Mr. Beemer asked Miss de Rozier to pose in her balloon as publicity for his hotel.

VALLIER: What did she have to say?

THE COUNTESS: Three months ago, just before her departure, she met your father.

VALLIER: I can only hope you're telling the truth.

THE COUNTESS: I would never make up such a story. Ask Timothée.

TIMOTHÉE: The Countess is tellin' the truth. The young lady says she seen your father, Count de Tilly, in a salon in Paris.

VALLIER: What else did she say?

THE COUNTESS: Many more people have joined the ranks of the royalists. Émile Combes, that dreadful man responsible for our fleeing to Canada, resigned. And his law denying the clergy any power in the schools has been challenged. Your father is at the head of this movement. The dissolution of the Third Republic and the return of a new monarchy are imminent. [*Gently.*] Your father will be coming back to get us so we can attend the coronation of Philippe VIII. [*Beaming.*] We left France, with the loyalist religious orders, like fugitives, but we shall return as conquerors!

VALLIER: How marvelous!

THE COUNTESS: I promised the young lady that you would stop by the Hôtel Roberval to thank her.

VALLIER [*preoccupied*]: If we go back to France, will we take Timothée with us?

THE COUNTESS: Timothée has been your footman for six years. We couldn't possibly manage without him. One doesn't change footmen the way one changes one's socks. [*She finds herself quite amusing but says no more.*] Really!

VALLIER: And Simon....

THE COUNTESS: He'll go wherever his father goes.

TIMOTHÉE: If you think I'd leave my Simon here, you're off your rocker! [*The* COUNTESS *and* VALLIER *are startled by* TIMOTHÉE's *language.*] On her deathbed, my poor departed wife made me promise I'd give Simon nothin' but the best, 'cause he was the best, the most beautiful child ever born since our Saviour. Just before she drew her last breath, I promised her he wouldn't lead the miserable poor life we led. That boy's my pride and joy. And any man's gonna want to take his pride and joy to Paris, the most beautiful city in the world. [*Laughter.*]

VALLIER: Finally some good news.

TIMOTHÉE: When do we leave?

THE COUNTESS: How impatient you are, Timothée!

FATHER SAINT-MICHEL *enters.*

THE COUNTESS: Good evening, Father Saint-Michel.

FATHER SAINT-MICHEL: Good evening, Countess. Good evening, Mr. Doucet.

THE COUNTESS: I have wonderful news! My husband is returning and will be able to attend your performance. What extraordinary theater! I finished Vallier's costume. I'm afraid it's more beautiful than Saint Sebastian's.

FATHER SAINT-MICHEL: You needn't work on them any more, Countess. I doubt that *The Martyrdom of Saint Sebastian* will ever see the light of day in Roberval.

THE COUNTESS: More of the same problems as last year, Father? And yet, in spite of Saint Alphonse's fall, you did have permission to start over again this year?...

FATHER SAINT-MICHEL: The problem is more complicated than that, and I'd rather not involve you in it.

VALLIER: Mrs. Bilodeau and her friends spoke to the principal?

FATHER SAINT-MICHEL: Among others. They were simply the fourth group of parents to show up in his office today. He's been such a faithful ally, but there's no way he can continue to defend my artistic projects. He's sending me on a retreat at the Mother House in Quebec City. I feel utterly defeated!

VALLIER: Father Saint-Michel, do you believe in your play?

FATHER SAINT-MICHEL: Of course I do!

VALLIER: Then why don't you try to conquer the unconquerable?

THE COUNTESS: Vallier is right. It's such a pity my husband won't get to see your play. I saw just a bit of it when I arrived here and it seemed so bold, so modern! Vallier was reciting: "Love! Love!" And Simon—your son, Timothée— was passionately kissing the young Bilodeau boy. But I probably have the line all wrong.

TIMOTHÉE [*threateningly*]: Father, maybe you could help the Countess tell us exactly what was going on? I'd really like to know myself.

FATHER SAINT-MICHEL: I think Vallier can be of more help to you than I can.

TIMOTHÉE: Monsieur, what was Simon doing with Bilodeau?

VALLIER [*innocently, but....*] He ... he was standing very close and speaking to him ... but the poor saint can barely hear him through the clamor of the celestial voices, and the archer has to bend over him to make himself heard.

THE COUNTESS: We can't possibly be talking about the same scene, Vallier. Or you're simply trying to minimize the intensity of Father Saint-Michel's staging. I saw it! Simon was kissing Bilodeau with a passion that would make all the ladies in Roberval blush with envy. It is Great Art!

TIMOTHÉE: Madame, Monsieur, you'll have to excuse me. I wanta have my own little artistic chat with my kid. [*Calling.*] Simon! Simon! Simon! [*He exits.*]

THE COUNTESS: Even Timothée seems to be carried away by your art. You have accomplished great things, Father Saint-Michel. We are going to miss you. Aren't we, Vallier? [*Silence.*] Vallier? Don't tell me you're off on the Mediterranean again.

VALLIER *exits, running.*

THE COUNTESS: We must get back to the manor and prepare everything for your father's return.

FATHER SAINT-MICHEL *puts the chair back.* THE COUNTESS *exits.*

THE STUDENT [*playing* THE SYRIAN SLAVE GIRL]: He is dying, the beautiful Adonis. Weep.... Too soon?

FATHER SAINT-MICHEL: Too late!

They exit. TIMOTHÉE *enters.*

TIMOTHÉE: Simon!

BILODEAU *enters.*

BILODEAU: You lookin' for Simon, Mr. Doucet? I think I know where you can find him.

TIMOTHÉE: Get out of my sight, you!

BILODEAU: How come? I got nothing to do with it. You can blame it all on Father Saint-Michel and his Antichrist performances. Anyway, we won't have to worry about the Antichrist any more. And people will stop laughin' at me 'cause I always havta play the girls' parts.

TIMOTHÉE [*calling*]: Simon, where the hell are you! Simon!

BILODEAU: It's none of my business, but you're gonna scream your lungs out for nothin' if I don't show you the way to the attic.

BILODEAU *exits, followed by* TIMOTHÉE.

BISHOP BILODEAU: You are debasing the most precious thing a human being has: his adolescence. The true genesis of adult life. You're turning me into a monster of pettiness.

SIMON IN 1952: That's the way you wrote it. We're just tellin' your story, Bilodeau!

BISHOP BILODEAU: I don't know what you're talking about! I want proof!

SIMON IN 1952: Be patient.

Episode 2

A week later.
The terrace of the Hôtel Roberval. SIMON *enters with* BARON DE HÜE,
*a doctor. The latter sits down at a table while the former remains
standing. At another table:* MADEMOISELLE LYDIE-ANNE DE ROZIER, *a
woman of about thirty, very elegant. In the distance, hovering in the
blue mist, a balloon.* BARON DE HÜE *gives* SIMON *a jar of ointment.*

BARON DE HÜE [*gazing off in the distance*]: That aerostat is mag-
nificent. I've seen a lot of them in my travels, but never one
with such flamboyant colors.

SIMON: The owner of that balloon took the deputy for a ride.
Guess it was the only solution.... Everybody was talking
about the balloon and forgot all about him. [*He laughs. Suddenly serious.*] I put this on three times a day, Doctor?

BARON DE HÜE: That's correct.

SIMON: Where there are still scabs?

BARON DE HÜE: Yes.

SIMON: You're sure the scars will never go away?

BARON DE HÜE: You'll have them for the rest of your life.

SIMON: I'd like to go for a balloon ride too, but I'd get the hell
outta here, forever!

BARON DE HÜE [*trying to comfort him*]: My wife, Sylvia, has gone
fishing with your father. I'd like you both to join us for dinner as soon as they return.

SIMON: No, I can't....

BARON DE HÜE: Good old Timothée. If he hadn't sent us that ca-
blegram, my wife would have missed a sensational fishing
season. [*Pause.*] I wonder why he sent you to me?

SIMON: You know, around here, we only got old Doctor Claveau with his horse remedies that taste so awful, and his
ointments that burn so bad, you figure they gotta be good
for you! [*He laughs nervously.*]

BARON DE HÜE [*suddenly solemn*]: You can confide in me, I'm a doctor.

LYDIE-ANNE [*from her table*]: Don't you feel, Baron, that you doctors tend to get carried away with your self-appointed right to always know and always tell the truth? "I'll be frank. You have a year left to live." "Your sickness is incurable." It's only a matter of time before the patient sinks into despair, defeat and prayer. What I call the deadly effects of the truth. While a tiny lie on your part could brighten up their dying days.

BARON DE HÜE: Can't you see I'm with a patient, Madame?

LYDIE-ANNE: I didn't realize the medical profession had abandoned their gloomy offices in favor of sunny terraces. [*She withdraws.*]

SIMON [*lowering his voice*]: I got a bit of money. I hope it's enough to pay for the ointment.

BARON DE HÜE: That won't be necessary. [*Pause.*] Perhaps it's hard for you to talk about it, but I want you to know that there are ways of preventing such abuse. Even here.

SIMON [*impulsively*]: I already told you! [*Correcting himself.*] No, I forgot to tell you. [*Hesitating.*] I fell ... off a horse ... onto some barbed wire. And I was goin' so fast, I kept rollin' over and over ... so I ended up with cuts all over my back.

BARON DE HÜE: You rolled over barbed wire and you only have cuts on your back?

LYDIE-ANNE *leaves her table.*

LYDIE-ANNE [*to* BARON DE HÜE]: May I? [*Without waiting for an answer, she sits down.*] This delightful breeze carries every sound, and I couldn't help but overhear your conversation. Allow me to say, young man, that you are a very bad liar, and it's a pity. With your looks you could be devastating.

BARON DE HÜE: Madame!

LYDIE-ANNE [*to* BARON DE HÜE]: He began by contradicting himself: "I already told you." "No, I forgot to tell you." A lie simply must begin with a positive sentence, not too emphatic, perhaps followed by a "Goodness, I forgot to tell you...." [*She laughs.*] It should put the person you're lying to in a position where he or she must participate in the lie: "Need I say?" Or be preceded by a compliment: "With your awareness of these things, you don't need me to tell you what you already know." And you carry on.... But you must avoid the kind of hesitation you just showed.

BARON DE HÜE: Do you always take people for simpletons? Do you really think a doctor can't tell whether cuts are made by barbed wire?

LYDIE-ANNE: I must point out that I was missing some of the details of the lie, but allow me to make up for it. Young man, why are you hiding the cause of your wounds?

SIMON [*angrily*]: It's none of your business. [*Suddenly sad.*] It might spoil your lovely vacation, Madame!

LYDIE-ANNE [*gently*]: You see that aerostat? It's mine. I got it in exchange for a few white lies. If I can ever be of any assistance ... I would be delighted....

SIMON: Be careful, Madame. I might take you at your word.

They stare at each other. Long silence. VALLIER *appears on the terrace.*

VALLIER: Simon!

LYDIE-ANNE: You are interrupting, young man.

VALLIER: Pardon me!

SIMON: What are you doing here?

VALLIER: An errand for my mother.

LYDIE-ANNE: Undoubtedly another patient for you, Doctor. Soon you'll need a nurse to assist you.

VALLIER: I went to see you, but your father told me that you were sick and couldn't have visitors. [*Silence.*] I thought that you'd at least come out to say goodbye to Father Saint-Michel. [*Pause.*] And what about the fire at the train station?

SIMON [*indifferent*]: I wasn't sick.

VALLIER: Timothée lied?

BARON DE HÜE [*sarcastically*]: Ah, it would seem that you have a disciple, Madame. I wonder what his approach is. He seems to have been convincing.

LYDIE-ANNE: You really don't want to understand my philosophy, do you? I landed in Roberval, expecting to meet a few Indians with war paint and feather headdresses. Just imagine my surprise when I met a real lady, not from the recent Napoleonic nobility, no, a true aristocrat, stranded in this....

VALLIER: You must be Mademoiselle de Rozier.

LYDIE-ANNE: That's the second time you've interrupted me, young man.

VALLIER [*happy*]: Pardon me. Please continue.

LYDIE-ANNE: She came up to me and asked whether I knew her husband, Count de Tilly.

SIMON: So she got you too, eh? The minute a Frenchman arrives in Roberval, the Countess pounces on him like a cat on a mouse, asking if he's seen her husband.

Hurt, VALLIER *says nothing.*

LYDIE-ANNE: The woman's situation is fascinating. Within five minutes I knew all her troubles. Her appearance betrayed her misfortune ... her dress is several summers out of style. Her face is the face of someone who never has enough to eat. When she told me she has been hoping for some news from her husband for five years now, it was all I could do not to burst into tears.

SIMON: You find that sad?

LYDIE-ANNE: I was devastated.

SIMON: Well, people round here make fun of her. They think it's pretty funny, the way she takes her shack for a castle and thinks all the surrounding countryside belongs to her. The way she calls Lac Saint-Jean "the Mediterranean."

LYDIE-ANNE: So I talked to her about her husband. I pretended that I had met him in some of the most fashionable salons in Paris. I dug up gossip about a few old fallen barons and dead viscountesses forging some utopian revolution. You should have seen the look on her face, her smile, when I told her I had connections in Paris who could get news to her husband. I brightened up her day. Her son is supposed to bring me some letters.

VALLIER: Here are my mother's letters, Mademoiselle de Rozier. I hope you'll have the decency to tear them up in front of me. You should be ashamed of lying to a poor woman....

LYDIE-ANNE: I should be ashamed? I made your mother happy, something which hadn't happened to her for five years. And I should be ashamed? Her happiness will last as long as this lie. Unless, of course, you insist upon distressing her.... [*She tears up the letters.*]

VALLIER: I'd like to talk to you in private, Simon. [*He puts his hand on* SIMON*'s shoulder.*] Simon?

SIMON [*aggressively*]: Get your hands off me!

BARON DE HÜE: Do you see where lying leads, Madame?

LYDIE-ANNE: You don't seem to understand, Doctor. These boys have a problem with the truth. Their eyes betray them. A pity that you work only on bodies. If you cared ever so slightly about the soul, you would see what I see.

BARON DE HÜE: You'll have to excuse me. I'm beginning to find the spring breeze tiresome. Simon, don't forget to tell your father I want to talk to him. [*He goes back into the hotel.*]

LYDIE-ANNE: I'll go along with you. I loathe moments of truth. Do wait for me, my friend. [*She catches up with* BARON DE HÜE.]

VALLIER [*worried*]: The whole village is over at the school. At the last minute, the principal assembled a choir to replace our play. We would have been performing *The Martyrdom of*

Saint Sebastian at this very moment. The deputy arrived
from Quebec City at noontime. The whole village turned out
to greet him. And I stayed home with my mad mother. I was
too unhappy. I missed you.

SIMON [*mean*]: So now you're gonna cry?

VALLIER: I don't understand why you ridiculed my mother.

SIMON [*lifting his shirt to show his back to* VALLIER]: Look at that,
Vallier! You want to see my ass too? See how it looks, thanks
to your goddam mother....

VALLIER [*appalled*]: Oh, my God! Did Timothée do that?

SIMON: That's right. My father did that to me. Thanks to your
  mother's blabbing about what I did to Bilodeau. I really
  liked the brave way you defended me. Shit, you could've
  made up something to confuse your mother. He was like a
  mad dog when he found me. He grabbed me by the arm
  and dragged me home. The minute we got inside the house,
  he went crazy. He pulled out all the dresses we kept after
  my mother died and he yelled: "Is this how you want to
  dress? Is that it?" He tied me to the bed while he drank his
  bottle of gin.... Then he took off his belt. "How many arrows did your goddam saint get?" [*Pause.*] I passed out a
  couple of times, but he kept swingin' away till I got my
  twenty-two lashes. And he hit hard, really hard. Harder and
  harder. Again and again.

VALLIER: Oh, beloved. Oh, loved one!

SIMON: Lucky only the train station burned down, 'cause I finally got hold of myself. Shit! I could've set all of Roberval
  on fire.

VALLIER: I shall have Timothée punished.

SIMON: You're gettin' as crazy as your mother, Vallier. The only
  reason my father ever shows up at your place is that he
  keeps dreamin' some day you'll take him to Paris. Your
  mother hasn't paid him for three years. He even gives you
  all your firewood every winter, and whenever we have

some supper left over, he takes it to you, like the other neighbors. "I shall have Timothée punished." You're as crazy as she is.

VALLIER: I forbid you to say that! She's not crazy. She's just playing her part. She's playing her part. She never could have survived the poverty and the isolation we've had to endure since my father left us, if she hadn't believed in her stories.

SIMON: You find that normal? You're gettin' as crazy as her, sayin' what you did to Bilodeau, about the two of us....

VALLIER: Simon, let's go down to the lake.

SIMON: Don't you understand? I don't want to have anything to do with you. It's all over. The attic, the hayloft, the closets, the lake! Don't you understand? Every time I go off with you, I'll be risking another beating. It's time for me to start thinkin' about girls.

VALLIER: I had a letter for you, too. I'd rather tear it up. [*He tears up the letter and puts it back into his pocket.*]

SIMON: Vallier, try to understand. I havta think about girls. Now don't start crying. I hate it when you cry.

BILODEAU *enters.*

BILODEAU: Simon, Mademoiselle de Rozier wants to buy you a liqueur. And you, Lily-White, go play somewhere else. My father's the manager and he says this is no place for beggars.

VALLIER *leaves.*

BILODEAU [*to* SIMON *as he passes him the drink.*] She'd like to talk to you.

SIMON: Get lost, Bilodeau.

BILODEAU: I just wanted to do you a favor. When you're married to some nice fat local girl and you havta spend your life shovelling sheep shit and cow manure to feed your fourteen kids, you'll remember the chance you had here on the terrace of the Hôtel Roberval. [*Pause.* SIMON *downs the cognac.*] Dontcha know how to say "Thanks"?

LYDIE-ANNE *enters.*

LYDIE-ANNE: Well, here I am, as arranged.

SIMON: What?

LYDIE-ANNE: Didn't we agree that I would wait until you had finished your conversation before joining you?

SIMON: I never said that.

LYDIE-ANNE: And yet, I did wait. Whether it's true or false, I did wait.

SIMON: So am I supposed to feel happy, like the Countess?

LYDIE-ANNE: Now you're defending her?

SIMON: I don't like goin' around talkin' about people.

LYDIE-ANNE: What I dislike most about this two-horse town is that no one ever says anything bad about anyone. Take that boy! [*Pointing to* BILODEAU.] He can't stop singing your praises.

SIMON: You two make a fine pair of liars!

LYDIE-ANNE: People here are so good, so generous and so absolutely kind.

SIMON: We can't afford to spend all day gossiping. We got work to do, Madame.

LYDIE-ANNE: Except for you. You have the hands of a gentleman.

SIMON: What does that mean?

LYDIE-ANNE [*takes his hands in hers gently*]: They're so soft and silky and white!

BILODEAU *exits.*

LYDIE-ANNE: I like your adolescent manner, awkward but passionate. I like the look in your eyes. At this point, I like everything about you. I'd even like to have you spoil my vacation.

SIMON: Well, I'm not so sure you'd like my back.

LYDIE-ANNE [*gently lifting up* SIMON*'s shirt*]: Whatever could you have done to deserve such punishment?

SIMON: I kissed ... someone.

LYDIE-ANNE: Is that so terrible?

SIMON: I guess so.

LYDIE-ANNE [*takes the jar of ointment from* SIMON]: This pomade will do you a world of good. Would you like me to apply it? Such intolerance! And this someone you kissed was the young man who just left? The Countess's son?

SIMON: Did Bilodeau tell you that? [*Silence.*] Not so hard, it hurts.

LYDIE-ANNE: I know that you have kissed him. I have never seen two young men look at each other so intensely. I can understand why you're attracted to him. He's very seductive. Which is more than one can say for the young girls around here ... they tend to be a bit on the plump side.

SIMON: That's not true. There's lotsa pretty girls around, Madame, and they don't havta wear a suit of armor around their middles to look thin. I bet you've got marks on your back by the end of the day too!

LYDIE-ANNE [*laughing*]: You're obviously not used to talking to women. You have a most unusual approach to seducing them. So then, did you or didn't you kiss that young man?

SIMON: The only one I ever kissed was Bilodeau, and that was just to piss him off.

LYDIE-ANNE: I can tell you're lying.

BILODEAU *enters.*

SIMON: I'll show you if I'm lying. [*He kisses* LYDIE-ANNE *vigorously.*]

BISHOP BILODEAU AND YOUNG BILODEAU: No!

BISHOP BILODEAU: I refuse to witness such debauchery!

BILODEAU: This is a terrace, not a bedroom!

SIMON: The worst thing that can happen is that I'll get another whipping. They can just follow the scar marks.

LYDIE-ANNE: You needn't fear a thing. With me, you're not risking the whip. A lie or two maybe. But not the whip.

BILODEAU [shocked]: This is a terrace, a terrace.... [He exits.]

BISHOP BILODEAU [carried away]: It was the hotel's main terrace. Nobody could get away with that kind of kiss in public. It simply wasn't done.

SIMON IN 1952: You're startin' to believe in your own story?

Silence.

Episode 3

Late August, 1912.
The de Tillys' house. Night. THE COUNTESS's *living room is in a deplorable state. A few worn pieces of furniture here and there. She is in her dressing gown, fussing over some plants in a planter filled with earth. There is a fire raging on the other side of the street.*

THE COUNTESS [*humming*]: "Heure exquise." Ask me to dance, Philippe Antoine. [*Pause.*] Such a small pleasure to grant your wife. Oh, I see! You're worried about this fire? It's only the old convent and, as usual, our valiant fire brigade will succeed in saving the foundation. Ever since Father Saint-Michel left three months ago, the only excitement in Roberval is these fires and the deputy's visits. So, shall we dance? Very well, I'll ask Timothée. I'll make you jealous. [*She dances alone, humming more loudly. She stops dancing abruptly. Concerned.*] Timothée, do you think he'll come back?

Knocking. THE COUNTESS *goes to open the door.*

BILODEAU: Evening.
THE COUNTESS: What are you doing here?

BILODEAU *enters.*

BILODEAU: I was helpin' them put the fire out and I decided to take a few minutes off to visit Vallier.
THE COUNTESS: You know very well you are the last person on earth Vallier wishes to see.
BILODEAU: He thinks I'm the one who broke up his friendship with Simon. I just want to have a talk with him. Especially 'cause I got some good news about Simon. He's gonna get married, to rich Mademoiselle de Rozier.

THE COUNTESS: Simon is getting married?

BILODEAU: That's right, and they're not wastin' any time. No wonder. After all the smooching they've done for the last three months. All that parading around, exchanging their wet kisses on the sidewalks, in the stores, even on the steps of the church ... it was indecent. Roberval was beginning to feel like Babylon. The engagement party is tomorrow evening on the terrace where they met.... Nice, eh? And afterwards, they're leavin' for Paris. Guess we won't be seeing Simon around these parts very often, eh? He'd really like to see you at his party, you and Vallier.

THE COUNTESS: You've been hiding this from me, Timothée. [*To* BILODEAU.] I shall tell my son. It seems to me you could be of help over there ... with the fire.

BILODEAU [*as he exits*]: You're gonna come, right? And you'll tell Vallier about Simon?

THE COUNTESS: Without fail.

BILODEAU *exits.*

BISHOP BILODEAU [*beaming*]: How can you claim that I announced your engagement to the Countess? You weren't there. Once again, all of that is untrue.

SIMON IN 1952: I got all of these scenes from you. [*He picks up a small notebook and reads.*] "The convent had been burning for hours. Felt like that fire was inside me too. I don't know why, but I had to go tell Lily-White that Simon and the Babylonian were getting married. It was my mother who called Lydie-Anne 'that woman from Babylon.' Suddenly I knew Lily-White was the only person in the world who could prevent Roberval from becoming another Babylon ."

BISHOP BILODEAU: Who wrote that?

SIMON IN 1952: You! It's your diary.

BISHOP BILODEAU: And how could you have such a diary in your possession?

SIMON IN 1952: Your memory's failing with age.

VALLIER *appears in his nightshirt.*

THE COUNTESS: Did I awaken you? You should have slept in the South Wing of the manor tonight.

VALLIER: Oh, so now we have a south wing?

THE COUNTESS: Of course. I've decided to call it the Wing of Hope. Do you like it?

VALLIER: Yes. It's a fine name.

THE COUNTESS: Tomorrow the architects are coming to see about the North Wing. It must be ready before your father returns. I was thinking of calling it the Wing of the Home-coming. I'm glad the old convent is on fire, it blocked the view of our manor house. Shall we dance?

VALLIER: No, I'm exhausted from my day on the lake.

THE COUNTESS: You are always exhausted. Where is your ener-gy, my son? Where? I watch you grow and all I can say is— you are growing and it is exhausting you. A centimeter here, a centimeter there, and there's nothing more to be said. Ever since your falling out with Simon, you have become as elu-sive as your reflection on the Mediterranean. Are you sure you won't dance?

VALLIER: I'm going to bed.

THE COUNTESS: It's not by going to bed now that you're going to know how to dance at Simon's engagement party. [*Silence. Realizing she has hurt him.*] Mrs. Bilodeau's son stopped by to invite us to the party.

VALLIER [*disturbed*]: I won't be going.

THE COUNTESS: Vallier! Your best friend is getting married and you won't even pay him the courtesy of attending his en-gagement party?

VALLIER: I'm going to sleep in the Wing of Hope. I have to get up early tomorrow.

THE COUNTESS: Just what do you intend to do tomorrow? Spend another day "meditating" on the Mediterranean? I never see you any more. You leave the house at dawn and come home after dark. And furthermore, you've been neglecting your appearance. You are a count, Vallier. I noticed your hands at the dinner table: they are beginning to look like the hands of a laborer.

VALLIER: I have noticed yours as well. You come back from your horticultural sessions with your hands all scraped and rough, your face stained with earth, mud in your hair, grit in your mouth....

THE COUNTESS [*evasive*]: Timothée told me the nuns barely had time to finish their evening prayers.... You missed the spectacle, Vallier, all the young novices running into the street half nude....

VALLIER: You are so good at avoiding subjects you find unpleasant. I think it's time I revealed the reason for my long days on the "Mediterranean," as you would say. Since my hands have already betrayed me, I won't try to hide it from you any longer. But, please, promise me you won't scream.

THE COUNTESS: As if I constantly went around screaming! Timothée, some linden tea please. [*She sits down.*] I am listening.

VALLIER: Ever since I finished school, I have been working with the Indians as a fishing guide.

THE COUNTESS [*in a grave voice*]: Never in the history of France has a Bourbon worked.

VALLIER: We are no longer part of that world.

THE COUNTESS: And you expect me not to scream?

VALLIER: Stay calm, I beg of you.

THE COUNTESS: How can you expect a mother to calmly accept that her son, a direct heir to the throne of France, a possible

Dauphin, is working? Working! The most vile, the most infamous of all occupations for an aristocrat. And you, my son, have stooped so low as to become a guide for tourists.... A valet? A porter? A savage?

VALLIER: Yes, Mother!

THE COUNTESS: I shall disown you. You are a coward! A coward like your father! [*She falls silent as if she just said something unspeakable.*]

VALLIER: I didn't hear the end of your sentence. [*Silence.*] Would you mind repeating it?

THE COUNTESS [*abruptly*]: Don't you want to learn how to waltz?

VALLIER: Would you mind repeating your sentence?

THE COUNTESS: Shall we waltz?

VALLIER: Timothée, what did my mother say?

THE COUNTESS: He's down in the kitchen.

VALLIER: I'm afraid you're wrong. [*Silence.*] Thank you, Timothée. That's what I thought she said. You can go back to the scullery now and feed the rats. [*Pause.*] You are truly unique, Mother. Most people allow their past to become foggier over the years.

THE COUNTESS: Who would dare claim that Count Philippe Antoine de Tilly is a coward?

VALLIER [*angrily*]: Who would dare claim that a man, and a Bourbon at that, who left his wife and his son without a cent in some remote region of Canada, who returned to France to play at Twentieth-Century Crusades, a man who didn't contact his family once in five years to let them know if he was dead or alive—who would dare claim that such a man is a coward? Well, Mother, I dare make such an audacious claim. I have ten times more courage than him. If I hadn't been secretly working since I was thirteen years old, we would have perished a long time ago. He is a coward! A coward! A coward like all men.

THE COUNTESS: You speak with the voice of anger. I prefer to believe what you wrote.

VALLIER: What do you mean?

THE COUNTESS: That letter.

VALLIER: What letter?

THE COUNTESS: The one I found in the drawer of your Louis-Philippe writing desk. I caught the chambermaid searching through your personal effects. I dismissed her on the spot. [VALLIER *runs towards his room.*] There was a torn letter. I wanted to put it back into the drawer, but inadvertently the word "love" caught my eye. I understood immediately that it was a letter to your father.

VALLIER [*offstage*]: Where is the letter?

THE COUNTESS: It is no longer here.

VALLIER [*offstage*]: Where is it?

THE COUNTESS: In good hands.

VALLIER [*returns*]: Whose good hands?

THE COUNTESS: I imagined how happy it would make your father to read that epistle. Perhaps I had no right, but my enthusiasm made me forget that I should respect your privacy. I glued the letter together. I took it myself to Lydie-Anne de Rozier so that she might send it off to her connections in France. [VALLIER *remains silent.*] Yes, I read it and you should be grateful to me. Your praise of the man of your life was overwhelmingly poetic. I couldn't hold back my tears when you said you missed him so terribly that you sometimes longed for death, like Saint Sebastian. [*She quotes.*] "You are my first love and you shall always remain so. Ever since our bitter separation, relentlessly, I re-create you, I compose you, I bring you to life, I kill you and resuscitate you. I miss you, your eyes of onyx, your skin of ivory, your body of marble. My breath comes too fast, for I have forgotten the rhythm of yours."

VALLIER AND THE COUNTESS: "My lips stumble on your name, for they have lost the habit of calling it. My hands reach out in the hope of your return, and are filled with nothing but my tears. Oh, beloved, if indeed you do love me, let your love be shown unto me. I love you and I shall wait for you forever."

THE COUNTESS: Do you think he will return? As you get older, you look more like him. Speak to me the way he used to speak to me.

VALLIER: I find him too cowardly to want to be like him. But I can understand the pain he's been through. And now I know that he tries to send me signals. These fires are signs of his suffering. [*Nods towards the blaze across the street.*] That fire is the sign that Mademoiselle de Rozier gave him my letter and he read it.

THE COUNTESS: But why associate this fire with your father? Vallier, I think I see something in your eyes, something other than filial love. Do you have another love? Tell me.

VALLIER: I am in love with Simon.

THE COUNTESS: You pronounce his name with such sadness.

VALLIER: I thought that you would be shocked.

THE COUNTESS: One must never confuse nobility and love. A state of the mind and a state of the soul.

VALLIER: How long have you known?

THE COUNTESS [*after a brief silence*]: I wanted to hear it from your lips. I have no one but you to cherish.

VALLIER [*smiling*]: And what about Timothée? And the chambermaid? The stable boys? And the kings and queens?

THE COUNTESS: And you, my great sea captain, whom I shall awaken early tomorrow morning, so that like a buccaneer he can guide the fishermen through the waters of the Mediterranean.

VALLIER *makes a move to exit.*

VALLIER: Good night, Mother.

THE COUNTESS: We must attend Simon's engagement party.

VALLIER: Why?

THE COUNTESS: To see whether he is the coward you say he is.

She looks towards the fire.

Episode 4

The following evening.
LYDIE-ANNE*'s and* SIMON*'s engagement party. The terrace of the Hôtel Roberval.* LYDIE-ANNE, *dressed in white, is surrounded by the guests:* BARON DE HÜE, *his wife* SYLVIA, TIMOTHÉE, THE COUNTESS, JEAN BILODEAU *who is serving, and finally* SIMON, *who stays close to* LYDIE-ANNE, *his fiancée as of several minutes ago.*

LYDIE-ANNE: ... And then, he took me into his arms, as if he had already held hundreds of women prisoners this way.... And there, on this very terrace, we were swept away in a torrent of embraces. And so we stayed, entangled in each other's arms, for three months. Meanwhile the budding trees of spring burst into blossom, from the sheer pleasure of spying on us. I traveled round the world searching for love....

Applause. SIMON *kisses her discreetly.*

LYDIE-ANNE: Such passion in public.
BILODEAU: Must be the champagne that's gettin' to you, eh, Simon?
THE COUNTESS: Charming Lydie-Anne, I do wish Father Saint-Michel could hear you now. He would have given you a wonderful role, "*la dame aux camélias*" perhaps.
BARON DE HÜE: She should have spent all three months on the terrace. Her pneumonia would have been much more convincing than the most sophisticated theatrical devices. [*Laughter.*]
LYDIE-ANNE: Truth will be your downfall, Baron.
BARON DE HÜE: I do hope I'll survive till your wedding.... Unless this is merely another lie?
LYDIE-ANNE: It would be the saddest of my career. We shall leave Roberval shortly, traveling by aerostat to Quebec City, and from there on to New York where we'll take the *Britannia* to Le Havre.

THE COUNTESS: How proud you look, dear Timothée.

TIMOTHÉE: I just wish my dear deceased wife was here to come along with us.

BILODEAU: My God, you're being morbid, Mr. Doucet.

TIMOTHÉE: I didn't mean to spoil the party.

BILODEAU [to TIMOTHÉE]: Would you please stop fillin' your glass so full! That's twice I had to wipe up.

LYDIE-ANNE: Would you please go to the kitchen and see whether the cake is ready, Bilodeau?

BILODEAU: Just wait a minute, till I finish serving.

THE COUNTESS: Simon, what an admirable father you have. [To the others.] I have never seen a father so devoted to a son. And so gentle and understanding.

TIMOTHÉE [uncomfortable]: I'm not so nice all the time, Countess. The Good Lord gives us children to bring them up proper and teach them about life. Sometimes you havta be tough to keep them on the straight and narrow, and....

THE COUNTESS: What do you mean, my good man? You, tough? I don't believe a word of it. Am I right, Simon?

LYDIE-ANNE [to save the situation]: My, you're talkative this evening, Countess. Your gown is ravishing. Those prints have become impossible to find these days. [To TIMOTHÉE.] So, my dear father-in-law, you are finally going to Paris?

TIMOTHÉE [relieved]: That's right, I'm finally gonna see the old country. I met so many Frenchmen since the hotel opened, it'll take me a year to go around visiting them all. I'm gonna take the grand tour. [He laughs.]

BARON DE HÜE: You'll have to come to see me too, Timothée. If only to finally tell me the name of the one who attacked your son!

BILODEAU [as he fills glasses]: My mother says you make a fine couple. She says you decided to get married pretty fast, but sometimes these things can't wait. Mrs. Lavigne and Mrs. Scott, they say you don't often see a woman of your age marry a nineteen-year-old kid, but we mustn't forget he lost his mother real young.

LYDIE-ANNE: We shall leave as soon as Simon finishes haying. If the mosquitoes haven't devoured him first.

BARON DE HÜE: Did you hear that, Sylvia? Mademoiselle de Rozier seems to share your aversion to mosquitoes.... Sylvia?

BARONESS DE HÜE: I'm still trying to imagine how someone managed to catch that enormous ouananich on the wall in the lobby. What were you saying? In your opinion, what kind of bait did the man who caught that monster use? Winchester fly bait or a salamander?

BARON DE HÜE: It depends upon whether he was alone or with his wife. If he was alone, he undoubtedly used a salamander. But if he was with his wife, I'm sure he used her as bait.

SIMON *is the only one to laugh. He quickly falls silent.*

BARONESS DE HÜE: Forgive me. I was still out on the lake.

THE COUNTESS: Just like my son. He loves the water. He can spend whole days, like you, Madame, out on the Mediterranean.

BARONESS DE HÜE: The Mediterranean? [*Polite coughing.*] Oh, the Mediterranean! And what does he catch?

THE COUNTESS: He doesn't go fishing. I believe he meditates on the return of ... of his father.

BILODEAU [*re-enters*]: It's true. Apparently Lily-White spends all his days out on the lake. Mrs. Scott and Mrs. Lavigne say he's turned wild like an Indian. Too bad he didn't come to your party!

BARONESS DE HÜE: How old is he?

THE COUNTESS: He'll be nineteen tomorrow, the same age as Simon.

BARON DE HÜE: Nineteen. The age where young men need to go on a retreat to think about women. How about you, Simon, where did you go on your retreat?

LYDIE-ANNE [*joking*]: To attics and haylofts and closets. Isn't that true, Simon? [*Silence.*]

BARON DE HÜE: The poor lad hasn't said a word since the party began.

LYDIE-ANNE: My dear doctor, young men are not given to talking about their retreats. You of all people should know that.

THE COUNTESS: I'd like to invite you all to the manor house tomorrow to celebrate my son's birthday.

BARONESS DE HÜE: Your manor is on the shore of the "Mediterranean"?

LYDIE-ANNE: Near the strait of Gibraltar, on Saint Joseph Street, just across from the ruins.

BARON DE HÜE: Which ruins? Those of the church, of Tremblay's General Store, or the train station? Roberval is in the process of disappearing beneath its ashes.

BILODEAU: This morning, the *Mistassini* burned, tied to the dock. Right, Simon?

LYDIE-ANNE: Don't smile so much, Simon, you might wrinkle your lovely skin.

SIMON [*exasperated, takes* LYDIE-ANNE *aside*]: Can I talk to you for a minute?

LYDIE-ANNE: I can't get used to his exuberance.

They withdraw to a small adjacent room.

SIMON: I can do without your comments on my past. Figure out some other way to have a good time.

LYDIE-ANNE: How? By trying to remember that you once kissed me on the terrace? In the stores? In the street? Only in public? I'd like you to know that a measly five seconds, here and there over the past three months, hardly constitute a good time. Between your visits to the doctor and your constant urge to go haying, I was free to pass the time lying to myself about what I can expect on our wedding night. I never would have guessed that hay grows so fast in Canada. If my calculations are correct, you've mown the same acres three times this month. Not to mention the wild strawberries, the raspberries, the hazelnuts and the blueberries, the choke-cherries and the juneberries. The way you've been going at it, there can't be a berry left within miles.

SIMON: Why can't you just have a good time like everybody else?

LYDIE-ANNE: Since when is everybody having a good time?

SIMON: Today's the most important day of our lives. Why is there always somethin' botherin' you?

LYDIE-ANNE: It must have been nicer with Vallier. [SIMON *takes her gently into his arms. She speaks sincerely.*] I thought I had forgotten that. I love you so much, Simon.

SIMON: I'm your man now.

TIMOTHÉE *enters.*

TIMOTHÉE: It's pretty embarrassing. Everybody can hear you arguing. C'mon, we're waitin' for you to cut the cake. [*Silence.* SIMON *wants to go, his father stops him.*] Simon....

SIMON: Go ahead without me, Lydie. I'll be right there. [LYDIE-ANNE *leaves.*] Now what do you want?

TIMOTHÉE [*feigning joy*]: It's the most beautiful day of your life, my son! [*Pause.*] Once we're on the other side of the ocean, you'll understand why I did what I did.

SIMON: Pa, do you remember when you used to say: "He's the most beautiful, the most beautiful child in the world"? You made me play Jesus as a boy. You made sure I got the lead roles in the school plays. And I always had to be the one to present the gifts and flowers to all the important people on all the important occasions in Roberval. Do you remember, Pa? You used to say: "If anyone touches him, if anyone ever lays a finger on him...." Remember? Do you really think crossin' the ocean is gonna make me forget?

TIMOTHÉE: It wasn't easy for me either, son.

SIMON: I suppose it was easier for me? When the balloon takes off for Quebec City without you and you see me waving bye-bye, then, goddammit, we'll see who it's gonna be hard for.

TIMOTHÉE: Let's go, you don't know what you're sayin'.

SIMON: I'm gonna go empty a bottle of gin. Then it'll be my turn to say I didn't know what I was doing.

They join the guests again. We hear the Wedding March played very loud. BILODEAU *comes rushing in with the cake.*

LYDIE-ANNE [*bitterly, to* SIMON]: As proof of my love, Simon, as long as this great love of ours lasts, I'll force myself never to lie again.

THE COUNTESS: What can she mean? As if she had ever lied.

BARONESS DE HÜE: Our young French fishing-guide learned from the Montagnais that at this time of the year great schools of ouananich swim downstream after spawning. Apparently sexual exhaustion makes them greedier than ever for the bait.

BARON DE HÜE: Darling, you're boring our friends with all this talk about the sexual mores of the salmon.

Laughter. VALLIER *enters, draped in crimson, gold and cream-colored curtains, and wearing a crown of leaves in his hair. Long silence due to general stupefaction. The orchestra massacres several bars of the Wedding March and falls silent.*

BILODEAU: Vallier!

LYDIE-ANNE: My God!

BARONESS DE HÜE: Why, it's our guide!

VALLIER [*confidently*]: I didn't want to dampen everyone's spirits. I thought for the longest time about how I might contribute to the celebration.

LYDIE-ANNE: You've certainly raised your mother's spirits, she's all smiles since you appeared.

SIMON *takes her by the shoulder.*

TIMOTHÉE: Okay, Vallier, I don't think you belong here.

THE COUNTESS: I must remind you, Timothée, you are speaking to Count de Tilly.

TIMOTHÉE: Looks like a scarecrow to me.

VALLIER: I am Caesar, and they have just brought before me the fair Sebastian who prefers another religion to mine. Do you remember your lines, Simon?

THE COUNTESS: We're finally going to see the play. Go on, children, we're listening!

VALLIER [*playing* CAESAR]: Greetings, beautiful young man. Greetings, archer with the hyacinth hair. I greet you, leader of my cohort in Emesa. You gather your robes about you like a virgin who fears rape or murder. Yet, I do not want to murder you. I want to crown you before all the gods. [*Pause.*]

SIMON [*playing* SEBASTIAN]: Caesar, I am already wearing a crown.

VALLIER [*playing* CAESAR]: I see no crown.

SIMON [*playing* SEBASTIAN]: You cannot see it, my lord, although you have the eyes of a lynx.

VALLIER [*playing* CAESAR]: Why is that?

SIMON [*playing* SEBASTIAN]: Other eyes are necessary, armed with a different virtue.

VALLIER [*playing* CAESAR]: Who are the magicians who assist you in these arts and teach you such marvels?

SIMON [*playing* SEBASTIAN]: I know no other art than prayer.

VALLIER [*playing* CAESAR]: I do not believe, I will not believe in the crimes you have been accused of, leader of my light cohort. You are too beautiful. Speak: have I not rewarded you with all the honors, benefits, ornaments, hours of glory and prestigious arms?

SIMON [*playing* SEBASTIAN]: Yes, my lord, you have been most generous with me.

VALLIER [*playing* CAESAR]: Bring me two crowns, one of anemones, the other of laurel. I want to crown the Morose Child and myself. [*He goes to embrace* SIMON.]

SIMON [*playing* SEBASTIAN]: Caesar, know that I have chosen my god. [*Silence.*]

THE COUNTESS: How touching! They are moved.

TIMOTHÉE: Simon, get him out of here!

VALLIER: And if I don't leave of my own free will, Timothée, will you show me the way with your whip?

TIMOTHÉE: Get him out of here, for Christ's sake.

BARON DE HÜE: I'm afraid I must take my leave. Should you ever come to Paris, don't show up at my door, Mr. Doucet. I never have liked child molesters. Come, Sylvia. [*They exit.*]

TIMOTHÉE: Get him out of here!

SIMON [*leading* VALLIER *gently*]: C'mon, Vallier, I'll walk you home.

LYDIE-ANNE: I'll go with you.

VALLIER: Why? Do you fear for your wedding night?

LYDIE-ANNE *slaps him violently.*

VALLIER [*to* SIMON]: You should find a less dangerous way of telling me you're unhappy. People are beginning to worry in Roberval.

LYDIE-ANNE: We shall leave Roberval at sunrise.

She exits. TIMOTHÉE *follows* LYDIE-ANNE. *As he leaves the ballroom,* SIMON *stops near* VALLIER, *but then exits.* BILODEAU *follows him.*

BILODEAU: So now are you proud of yourself, Lily-White? You spoiled everything. Now he's gonna leave even sooner. [*Catches up with* SIMON.] Simon!

They exit. THE COUNTESS *is left alone with* VALLIER.

THE COUNTESS [*to amuse* VALLIER *who laughs*]: I'm so glad you decided to come. It relaxed the atmosphere. The party was a deadly bore until you arrived. No one wanted to dance. I found Lydie-Anne quite out of sorts towards the end.

VALLIER: Mama?

THE COUNTESS: Her gown was superb. I noted the pattern.

VALLIER: Mama?

THE COUNTESS: I want to wear one just like it the day your father returns.

VALLIER: Mama, I am proud of myself.

THE COUNTESS: And I am proud of you too!

VALLIER *bursts into tears in his mother's arms.*

VALLIER: He's leaving at dawn.

THE COUNTESS [*to the other guests*]: It's been lovely ... don't forget....

They leave the terrace. BILODEAU *enters and starts putting away the chairs.* SIMON *enters.*

BILODEAU: Simon!

SIMON: Bugger off, Bilodeau!

BILODEAU: Is that all the thanks I get, after everything I done for you? If you don't want anything to do with Lydie-Anne any more, I'll get rid of her for you. Ever since the French count and his mother have been here, it's like they're trying to soil your soul. One day Mrs. Scott and Mrs. Lavigne and my mother, they said you were so beautiful, only a saint could be that beautiful. Before Lily-White came between the two of us, we were always together, 'cause I wanted to be friends with a saint.

SIMON: Christ, what do you want from me, Bilodeau? What do you want?

BILODEAU: It's simple. I just want to be your friend again. [*Hands him a small notebook.*] I brought you my diary. I wrote down everything I done to keep you pure. [SIMON *doesn't take the notebook.*] In two weeks, I'm leaving for the Seminary in Chicoutimi.... Don't leave with the Babylonian. Come with me.

BISHOP BILODEAU: This is pure defamation!

SIMON: Tomorrow I'm gonna be in a balloon that'll take me far far away. There's a lotta things I'm gonna miss, but at least I won't have you on my back any more.

BILODEAU: I have to save your soul!

BISHOP BILODEAU: Lies! Lies!

SIMON IN 1952: Later that night there was an enormous explosion in Roberval. It lit up the whole village. The sky glowed red for hours.

Episode 5

The following evening.
The de Tillys' house. The house is cluttered with makeshift decorations. There is a bathtub in the middle of the room.

THE COUNTESS: Surprise! Surprise!

VALLIER: A bathtub!

THE COUNTESS: Happy birthday!

VALLIER: You remembered!

THE COUNTESS: Of course. I had this bath set up for you. Are you pleased?

VALLIER [*undressing*]: How nice of you. You must have gone to a great deal of trouble.

THE COUNTESS: My son, your nakedness might embarrass our guests. Everyone is here. [*Introducing them.*] Madame the Baroness, Monsieur the Baron, Father Saint-Michel....

VALLIER: How nice of you all to have accepted my mother's invitation!

THE COUNTESS: ... And Simon. Aren't you going to kiss Simon? He's over there. On the divan.

VALLIER: I can imagine the divan, but Simon ... that's more difficult.

THE COUNTESS: Try!

VALLIER: I can't.

THE COUNTESS: Too bad. He'll arrive later then. [*Brings him a birthday cake.*] Make a wish, Vallier.

VALLIER: My cake! But it's made of earth?

THE COUNTESS: It's my favorite cake recipe.

VALLIER: I'm willing to be polite to all our guests, but having to eat earth....

THE COUNTESS: Children are so ungrateful....

VALLIER: We shouldn't involve our guests in family feuds. I am very touched by everything you've done for my nineteenth birthday.

THE COUNTESS: There's more to come, my son. Tomorrow we shall go fox-hunting. [*A knock at the door.*] A late guest!

She goes to open the door. SIMON *enters.*

SIMON: Good evening, Countess.

THE COUNTESS: Simon! How nice of you to come. You see, I told you he was here.

SIMON [*defensively*]: I was just passin' by, so I thought I'd stop in and wish you a happy birthday. And say goodbye.

VALLIER [*suddenly as strained as* SIMON]: What a fine idea to kill two birds with one stone. Lydie-Anne didn't come with you?

SIMON: No. She's back at the hotel. We got you a present. [*He hands him a package which* VALLIER *doesn't open.*] It's a book on the fish of Lac Saint-Jean. It just came out.

THE COUNTESS: You must thank Lydie-Anne. Vallier loves fish. [VALLIER *stares at his mother.*] Let's leave them alone for a moment. Come and visit the Wing of the Homecoming.

She exits with her phantom guests. Pause.

VALLIER: Have you noticed that I haven't cried since you came in?

SIMON: We're changing. We're getting older.

VALLIER: Yes. We understand life better as we get older. I felt a bit silly last night. The village ... the Indians haven't forgiven me. I lost my job this morning.

SIMON [*after a pause*]: You know, I felt pretty stupid myself on the terrace last spring.

VALLIER: We were young then. Now, we're older. You're going to be happy with Lydie-Anne. She's got character, she's beautiful and rich. I envy you. I won't be that lucky. I don't have the kind of looks that attract beautiful Amazons.

SIMON: Don't say things like that, Vallier. You're so nice, you're beautiful.

VALLIER *stands up in the tub and faces* SIMON.

VALLIER: Do you really think so?

Uncomfortable, SIMON *turns his back to him.*

SIMON: We're leavin' for Paris the day after tomorrow. Lydie-Anne has to settle the insurance business before we can leave. They still haven't found out who blew up the balloon. [*Pause.*] Can I wash your back?

VALLIER *sits back down in the tub.*

VALLIER: Stop. Go away!

SIMON: I'm not happy, Vallier.

VALLIER: Why not? You have everything a man could want in life. You should be ashamed of saying such a thing. There are people who live in misery and poverty and yet they always find a way to see the bright side of life.

SIMON: But, Vallier, I'm not sure this is what I want in life. I don't think I love Lydie-Anne the way I should.

VALLIER: It's normal to be nervous about it. You didn't know many women before her.

SIMON: Maybe you're right. Well, I better get going. Thanks for your advice.

VALLIER: You'll forgive me if I don't see you to the door. [*Pause.*] We're never going to see each other again. Trips from Roberval to Paris and back are few and far between, you know. If I judge by my father, they are very, very rare. [*Pause.*] When are you finally going to say it?

SIMON: I can't....

VALLIER: Try!

SIMON: What I feel for you is stronger than what I feel for Lydie-Anne.

VALLIER: What is it called?

SIMON [*with all the difficulty in the world*]: Love. I love you, Vallier.

VALLIER: I love you, Simon.

SIMON *jumps into the bathtub, dressed. They embrace each other, caress each other.*

BISHOP BILODEAU: No!

SIMON IN 1952: Look at them loving each other, Bilodeau. Look at them! Look at what made you sick in the school attic!

BISHOP BILODEAU: I beg of you!

VALLIER: That's new. You're crying now.

SIMON: You smell so good. So good! [*He caresses his face.*] When she slapped you, it felt like she had slapped me. [*Pause.*] It was real brave of you to blow up Lydie's balloon!

VALLIER: You mean, you're not the one who did it? [*They laugh.*]

SIMON: It's a sign that I should stay. My beautiful love!

They kiss passionately. THE COUNTESS *enters. They stop.*

THE COUNTESS: Not again! Aren't we ever going to get to see the end? Every time I come in, you stop. At the same point! And this kiss? [*Reciting.*] "Love! Love!" Go on!

SIMON: Are you sure?

THE COUNTESS: We want nothing more.

They embrace each other.

SIMON: I shall be reborn. My breath and the heavens bear witness. I shall be reborn.

VALLIER: We shall find sails filled with the rising wind, prows sharp as the desire for the good life! We shall be free. Glorious and free on the high seas. Oh, beloved. Oh, beloved.

SIMON: One must kill one's love that it may be reborn seven times more ardent. My destiny must be fulfilled. I must die at the hands of men.

LYDIE-ANNE *enters with* BILODEAU.

LYDIE-ANNE: And if it were at the hands of a woman, would that be acceptable?

THE COUNTESS: Lydie-Anne! Bilodeau! How nice.

BILODEAU: I told you he was here, didn't I?

LYDIE-ANNE: You vulture, Bilodeau!

THE COUNTESS [*whispering*]: Do sit down, the performance has begun.

LYDIE-ANNE: I've seen enough for the time being. So this is how you spend your evenings after haying, Simon? I never thought farmers wore so little clothing.

SIMON: Let me explain.

LYDIE-ANNE: There is nothing to explain. I was silly and ridiculous. I am in love. Now I shall know that love is the worst of all the lies one can tell oneself.

THE COUNTESS: What you said is very touching. What part are you playing?

LYDIE-ANNE: The woman betrayed, Countess, and in the theater one laughs at betrayed women.

THE COUNTESS [*laughing*]: It's true. They're usually so amusing when they express their astonishment.

LYDIE-ANNE: [*screaming*]: I am expressing my pain. Something no one here seems to understand.

THE COUNTESS: On the contrary. You are disarmingly convincing. Go on! Your acting is wonderful!

LYDIE-ANNE [*hurt*]: Did I talk about your pain, Madame? It's not obvious, but everyone makes fun of it. They say you are mad.

THE COUNTESS: What is she talking about?

LYDIE-ANNE: Should I have told you that I met your husband in Lyon? Should I have told you he is now mayor of a "commune"? Should I have told you the truth? That he had me to dinner with his charming young wife and their two delightful little girls? Should I have told you the truth so that we could see your pain? Should I have told you the truth? That men are liars ... and I too was lying ... to myself.

VALLIER *goes to his mother,* SIMON *towards* LYDIE-ANNE.

LYDIE-ANNE [*regains her composure*]: Don't touch me, Simon. We'll continue this discussion before the courts. I accuse you of destroying my aerostat.
SIMON: It wasn't me, Lydie!
LYDIE-ANNE: You kept your word, young man. You have ruined my vacation.

LYDIE-ANNE *exits.* SIMON *exits, followed by* BILODEAU.

SIMON: It wasn't me, Lydie! It wasn't me!
BILODEAU: Simon won't be leaving, Vallier! Simon won't be leaving!
VALLIER: Are you not feeling well, Mother. Are you all right?

THE COUNTESS *goes over to the cake and takes a mouthful.*

VALLIER: Stop punishing yourself like this! You mustn't believe everything she says.
THE COUNTESS [*grimly*]: Tomorrow morning, we shall go hunting as planned, and then, at noon, I shall be leaving you ... I shall be leaving ... for Paris.

Episode 6

The following noon, in the woods.

THE COUNTESS [*gaily*]: Faster! Faster! We must catch up with the
hounds! I saw them head south. We can't hear the lead dogs
barking any more. Stop.

VALLIER: Let's go on a bit farther. We'll head south and we shall
never stop again.

THE COUNTESS: No, here. I like this forest floor. I like the smell
of the earth.

VALLIER: Look over there. There's a hare caught in a snare.

THE COUNTESS: Is it still alive?

VALLIER: I think so.

THE COUNTESS: Don't kill it.

VALLIER: It's wounded.

THE COUNTESS: Then kill it!

VALLIER: You know that I would have great difficulty killing.

THE COUNTESS: Your every move must be merciless. Steady and
precise. Our entire life is revealed in the clarity and the
courage of our acts, Count de Tilly.

We hear bells in the distance.

VALLIER: I can hear the hounds returning.

THE COUNTESS: It's the bells of Saint Jean de Brébeuf. It's noon.

VALLIER: Already?

THE COUNTESS: The hour has come for me to return to Paris. I
feel a bit sad about leaving you.

VALLIER: I can't, Madame. I won't have the strength to go
through with it.

THE COUNTESS: Don't be like Sanaé refusing to give Saint Sebastian the eternity he longs for. "I shall be reborn, Sanaé. I
shall be reborn. But first I must die. If thou dost truly love
me...." Enough talk. The last ship for France will be leaving
soon. [*Moved.*] You were the only one who ever loved me in
my entire life. Who else could I ask this of?

VALLIER: Can love be that powerful?

THE COUNTESS: I believe it can. Please.

VALLIER: No, I refuse!

THE COUNTESS: Will you speak to me till the end?

VALLIER: Where will I find my strength if you abandon me?

THE COUNTESS: I leave you the manor house, all our land, the Mediterranean ... and all my love. Don't cry. Will you never get rid of this habit? We have to take leave of each other some day. It's the law of nature. Old trees must die so the sunlight can reach the young saplings. Their decaying bodies become new earth which is the finest legacy one person can leave to another.

VALLIER: No!

THE COUNTESS: Don't spoil my legacy. Stop crying, stop whimpering over your destiny. Play the part, Vallier, play the part.

VALLIER: I shall never cry again. I'll play the part, like you.

THE COUNTESS *lies down and covers her face with a veil.* VALLIER *begins to cover his mother with earth.*

THE COUNTESS: Talk to me. The images have all faded now. Tell me about your beautiful love for Simon.

VALLIER *stops covering* THE COUNTESS *with earth and begins to smother her.*

VALLIER: We met one winter morning. On the frozen lake. An immense white desert.... He lent me his coat. My European clothes didn't suit the climate.... I was cold ... but not him. The sun was blinding me ... but not him. I couldn't understand a word he was saying.... We were so different....

SIMON *suddenly arrives on the scene.*

SIMON: Vallier! I've been looking for you everywhere! [*Sees* THE COUNTESS *'s body.*] Come with me! We can't stay here!

They exit. We catch a glimpse of BILODEAU'S *silhouette flitting by.*

Episode 7

The following morning.
The attic of Saint Sebastian School for Boys. VALLIER *is sleeping in* SIMON*'s arms.*

SIMON: Wake up, Vallier. Look at the sunrise. I want you to see how beautiful it is. [VALLIER *wakes up.*] Look at the colors. There's nothing more beautiful than the sun rising over the lake.

VALLIER: Have you ever noticed the reflection of the sun on the water? The reflection is so delicate.

SIMON: Yes. The water makes the sun look like a beautiful, fiery lily. [*They embrace.*] We have to leave before daylight.

VALLIER: Why not stay here, in this attic, where it all started?

SIMON: Once they've searched everywhere else, they're gonna come lookin' here.

VALLIER: And what's the worst that can happen? The whip?

SIMON: No, Vallier. Death. An undeserved death. A horrible death because when they find your mother's body, they're not gonna see her suitcases and her joy to be leaving here, they're not gonna see how happy she is to be back in France at last. All they're gonna find in the woods is the body of a woman who was buried alive by her son.

VALLIER: I saw her in my dreams. She was waltzing on the banks of the Seine. I can prove to them that she is happy at last. I'll explain how I was able to give her this ultimate proof of my love.

SIMON: Nobody will believe you. They're too simple-minded to understand things they don't feel in their own lives.

VALLIER: But if you tell them, they'll believe you!

SIMON [*as he takes his wedding rings out of his pocket*]: I spent the whole summer pretending. I don't want to pretend any more, and I especially don't want us to pretend.

BILODEAU *enters.*

BILODEAU: I drove the buggy up close. I brought some food ...
and a gun ... for hunting.... You'll see, Simon, where we're
goin', nobody's gonna find us. That logging camp was
abandoned years ago. There's a little stream.... In the morning, when you get up, you see pheasants and foxes.... Looks
like a scene out of the Garden of Eden.... We'll make a new
life for ourselves. [*Pause.*] I'm so glad to be your friend now.
I'm so happy you've forgiven me. You're a real saint. That's
what they call "mercy." You're merciful, Simon. It was
worth it, eh, everything I did for you? It was worth blowin'
up Lydie-Anne's balloon, eh? [*Silence.*] Now you need me,
right? The only thing I'm gonna miss is when my mother,
Mrs. Lavigne and Mrs. Scott find out I left with the one who
killed his mother in the woods. I can just see their faces! I
won't be goin' to the Seminary.... It's more important to
dedicate my life to a saint.... We're gonna pray so hard....
We're gonna confess our sins.... We're gonna tell each other
all our bad thoughts....

SIMON *hands him a bundle.*

SIMON: Take this to the buggy! Hurry! They're gonna find us.
BILODEAU: Lily-White—Vallier—and me, we'll learn to get
along. I brought you back my diary. [*He hands it to him.*
SIMON *takes the diary and puts it into his pocket.*] Tell me you're
my friend.
SIMON: You're my friend, Bilodeau.
BILODEAU: You gonna give me a kiss?... Just a little saint's kiss?

SIMON *pushes him out the attic door.*

SIMON: Never, Bilodeau! Never! Never! [*He closes the door.*]
BILODEAU [*voice off*]: Open the door! Let me in!

SIMON *shows his wedding rings to* VALLIER.

SIMON: Here are my wedding rings.

VALLIER *takes one and swallows it.* SIMON *does the same.*

SIMON: Now, you're my lover, my man. My one and only love.
The sun and the lake are our only witnesses. For life, till
death do us part.
VALLIER: You are my love, my man. My ultimate love. For life,
till death do us part.
SIMON: This time I'm gonna find the courage. I'm gonna be as
brave as you. [*He picks up the oil lamp and smashes it on the
floor. Pressing* VALLIER *to him.*] I shall be reborn, Sanaé.
BILODEAU [*banging on the door*]: Simon, open the door! Don't
leave me alone! Simon!
VALLIER: Oh, Lord. One must kill one's love that it may be reborn, seven times more ardent.
SIMON [*suffocating*]: Give me your hands! Your hands!
VALLIER [*suffocating*]: If thou dost truly love me, let your love ...
be known unto me.

They collapse in each other's arms.

Epilogue

All the other actors come out onto the stage.

BILODEAU: Sodom! Sodom and Gomorrah!

BISHOP BILODEAU, *unable to restrain himself any longer, goes up onto the stage.*

BISHOP BILODEAU: It was Sodom and Gomorrah that was burning, and I was God, with the right to decide whether you would live or die.

SIMON IN 1952: Tell us the end of the story, Bilodeau! I passed out in Vallier's arms. When I woke up, I was in Doctor Claveau's office, with two policemen beside my bed. What happened while I was unconscious? What happened during those minutes that are missing from my memory? Those minutes that cost me the last thirty years of my life! Let's hear the end of your story, Bilodeau!

BISHOP BILODEAU: May God forgive me. May He grant me His mercy for the sacraments my hands have blessed. I couldn't understand the force that drew you together. The force that allowed you to overcome the beatings, a father's rejection, the public humiliation, a mother's death, the temptation of wealth and of a better life elsewhere.... A force so strong you were willing to die. I thought I could possess that force by running away with the two of you, but you rejected me right up to the last second. [*Pause.*] I finally managed to get the attic door open. Everything was on fire. You and Vallier were lying there in each other's arms, dying. I went up to you. The fire was coming closer and closer. I tore you out of Vallier's arms and dragged you away from the flames. I went back to get Lily-White but just as I got close to him ... I

Barnes & Noble Bookseller
1701 Sherman Ave.
Evanston, Il 60201
(847) 328-0883
01-20-03 S02520 R003

CUSTOMER RECEIPT COPY

Lilies, on the Revival   11.95
0887545459

SUB TOTAL   11.95
SALES TAX   1.02
TOTAL   12.97
AMOUNT TENDERED
VISA   12.97
CARD #:   ****************3011
AMOUNT   12.97
AUTH CODE   052421

TOTAL PAYMENT   12.97
        Thank you for Shopping at
        Barnes & Noble Booksellers
#134836 01-20-03 08:15P ChrisF

could hear your "never, never" echoing louder and louder. Never, Bilodeau! Never! Never! I turned on my heels and left him there. I closed the door behind me. It was Sodom and Gomorrah that was burning, and I was God, punishing you both by saving you and letting him die.

He goes to leave. SIMON *and the other actors block his way.*

SIMON IN 1952: Why didn't you let me die with him?

BISHOP BILODEAU: I wanted you to remember me. I wanted you to go on thinking of me, I didn't care how or what. When I testified against you, I knew that in prison you'd never stop thinking of me. And I succeeded. [SIMON IN 1952 *takes out his knife. The other actors follow suit.*] Oh, my archers, let my destiny be fulfilled. [*He opens his cassock.*] Let me die at the hands of men. Kill me! Kill me! I loved you so much I wanted to destroy your soul.

SIMON IN 1952 [*dropping the knife*]: I hate you so much ... I'm gonna let you live.

All the actors exit except for BISHOP BILODEAU, *who is left alone on stage.*

THE AUTHOR

Michel Marc Bouchard was born in 1958 in the village of Saint Coeur-de-Marie at Lac Saint-Jean, Quebec. At the age of fourteen, he organized his first tour of one of his own works, *Le Scandale*, through the tiny villages of Lac Saint-Jean. He has been an actor, director and theater administrator. The author of some twenty plays, he has been nominated twice for the Governor General's Award for Drama in French, in 1986 and 1990. In 1988, *Les Feluettes (Lilies)* was awarded both *le Prix littéraire du Journal de Montréal* and *le Prix du Cercle des critiques de l'Outaouais*.

THE TRANSLATOR

Linda Gaboriau lives in Montreal where she has been active in Canadian and Quebec theater for twenty years as a critic, journalist, broadcaster and consultant. She has translated more than twenty plays, including the works of some of Quebec's most prominent playwrights.

Cover Design: Stephanie Power / Reactor
Cover Illustration: Saint Sebastian (Andrea Mantegna)
Courtesy of Kunsthistoriches Museum, Vienna
Author Photograph: Robert Laliberté